Self-Discipline

The All-Inclusive Guide to Self-Discipline Mastery for Your Own Personal and Professional Success: Unleash Your Full Potential

(The Art of Self-Control: Harnessing the Power of Discipline to Transform Your Life and Achieve Unprecedented Success")

Sotiris Kontogianni

TABLE OF CONTENT

The Least Resistance Path 1
The Greatest Battle Is With Yourself 4
Learning The Most Recent Self-Regulatory Techniques 9
Apply The Rollover Technique 32
Quit Putting Things Off 44
Comprehending Self-Control 50
Do The Right People Not Require Inspiration? 67
Self-Discipline Habit 74
Getting Things Done: The Significance Of Self-Determination And Good-Habit Information .. 84
Tenacity And Self-Control 90
Dark Psychology In War 105
Saturday: Embracing Everything, Nothing Less 107
Ways To Respond To Failure 121

The Least Resistance Path

It's in our nature as humans to take the easiest route. Trouble—particularly when attempting to follow a diet, visit the gym regularly, or put in the extremely hard work required to learn a new skill or launch a new business.

Thankfully, this is something you can use to your advantage. As you can see, humans have a great deal of power over their surroundings. What is the path of least resistance that can be precisely adjusted? Water follows the path of least resistance when it flows downhill, but you can direct it in a different direction by digging a trench. Your life is the same way. It is possible to "outsource" self-control.

Let's examine a few instances.

Let's use the overused diet example for the first example, but you may use this technique for any aspect of your life where you want to "outsource" self-control.

So, how do you change your eating habits from bingeing on sweet, tasty junk food every night to sticking to porridge, vegetables, and boiled chicken? (Well, perhaps not to that extent, but you get the idea.)

It's shockingly easy to solve. You purge junk food from your home and replace it with solely wholesome foods; also, you never go shopping while you're hungry. You won't travel all the way to the store to get a chocolate bar, even if you have sugar cravings at home. The least-resisting route has shifted.

Forgive me for using yet another too-corny example, but let's say you frequently give in to the urge to watch TV after work. Let's imagine, instead, that you would like to make practicing the guitar a habit.

The answer remains the same. Adapt the least-restrictive route. Keep your TV remote hidden in the cabinet upstairs, and find another place to conceal the batteries. Next, set up your instrument somewhere convenient for you to get to, like on the kitchen bench or in the middle of the home. It will be simpler to practice guitar at home than to watch TV.

To change the route of least resistance in your favor, you modify your surroundings. You contract out your self-control. Decisions are made automatically.

Lesson: Try to make self-discipline as simple as you can.

In relation to automating choices, let's examine the opposite aspect of self-control: how to successfully "automate" your self-control and develop grit on autopilot.

The Greatest Battle Is With Yourself

Issues. They're in every place. These might be obvious concerns like poor health, financial difficulties, job-related stress, or a failing relationship. Even though you believe you are doing everything necessary and correctly, it appears like everything is crumbling around you.

Naturally, this could be more logical. You have the person of your dreams and are living the life you desire. You're working at the job you want. You work, but you are free to take breaks whenever you choose. You indulge in your favorite foods and pastimes. On paper, everything is wonderful.

However, you aren't genuinely happy, and we aren't living our lives on paper. Yes, of course, you are acting in a way that will dull your pain. You may be "wild and free" and go from job to job, drink, smoke, or see the people you want to see, which gives you the impression that you are happy, but deep inside, you aren't content with your life.

That persistent sense that something is lacking or that you could perform better in this or that area. You may wish to be more attractive, have a more satisfying relationship, or earn more money, but no matter how hard you work, you will never succeed in achieving your objectives.

Thus, why even bother?

For a moment, close your eyes and visualize a pitch-black road. There are yellow lines dotted around the paved area. Lamplights are lining the street so you can see, and it's a calm night with the moon and stars out.

You are jogging alone, the only person out here. You're sprinting hard and quickly. Though it is still quite a distance ahead of you, the finish is in sight. You feel exhausted and can barely breathe. You feel like giving up. Throw in the towel, then turn to leave.

"Is it really that important?" One asks oneself. Then, your inner critics begin to speak up and share their thoughts. "I'm worn out." "It's too difficult." "This feels awkward."

You may think of a plethora of reasons why you would lose motivation instantly. The more you consider it, the less motivated you are to put it to the test and the more you want to give up.

Doesn't it sound like the circumstances you are facing in your life? I want to present to you a paraphrasing of a statement made by Will Smith. "There is a small voice inside of you that says,

'I'm tired,' as you run. My lungs are about to burst. I can't possibly go on because I'm so hurt. And you'd like to give up.

You will learn how to keep going if you can overcome that individual while you're running. You'll persevere even when things in your life become difficult.

Yes, it is. When faced with hardships in life, giving up is the natural response. We are aware of the inner voice asking us to give up, get over it, and stop thinking about it. Who gives a damn about the outcome of this? For many people going through a difficult period, the most common thought is, "I'm just going to walk away."

However, you need to learn how to silence that small voice. I'm telling you that even though that voice could be questioning you if it matters if you finish the race, it does.

We encounter obstacles in life far too frequently, and we give up. We aspire to achieve, but when difficulties arise and terrible things occur, we are the first to throw up our hands and declare, "No one cares, so why bother?" Everybody has a small voice in them telling them to concentrate on the wrong things in life. This is the voice that drives our need always to get our way, to prioritize ourselves in all circumstances, and to do as we want. It is the voice that encourages us to disobey the law, not to follow timetables, and to do anything that contradicts our desires. It's the voice that instructs you to live your life "looking out for number" in order to be free.

Learning The Most Recent Self-Regulatory Techniques

You won't become disciplined by yourself overnight. It requires practice for days, weeks, months, or even years. It takes more than just setting objectives and giving up procrastination habits. You must put the following techniques into practice if you want to become an expert in self-control and fortify your will:

Acknowledge your shortcomings

It takes self-awareness to become a disciplined person. Are you having problems closing Facebook and other accounts that are a distraction? Do you need more patience? Are you unyielding or intransigent? Do you find it difficult to assign tasks? Are you overly perceptive? Do you need help to collaborate with others? It would help if you took the time to sit down and evaluate your deficiencies since they may prevent you from mastering self-discipline.

Recognizing your shortcomings is essential if you want to avoid performing poorly at work. Realizing and dealing with your defects enables you to reach your full potential. It provides you with the chance to transform these shortcomings into assets. Please put all of your flaws down on paper and devise a strategy for converting them into assets.

Delay your gratification.

Postponing satisfaction offers benefits. It makes you more grateful for what you already have. It instills in you the value of perseverance. Strengthens and disciplines the mind.

According to research by Walter Mischel from the 1970s, successful people are more likely to be able to postpone satisfaction. Dr.Mischel showed the kids a plate full of cookies during one experiment.

He gave the kids a few minutes to wait and promised a prize for the longest-lasting ones. After Mischel left the room, some kids gave in to their cravings and ate the cookies, but some kids managed to resist. Compared to children who ate cookies right away, those who were able to postpone gratification had superior academic results and fewer behavioral issues.

Being able to postpone happiness is necessary to develop into a very disciplined person. The following tactics will assist you in resisting the allure of instant satisfaction:

Recall your objectives.

Always remind yourself that there is something greater waiting for you at the end of the tunnel. Would you sacrifice the health of your lungs to enjoy two packs of smokes a day? Would you forfeit the chance to see the globe in exchange for a pricey designer purse? Are you willing to sell your lovely, lean figure for many slices of blueberry cheesecake? Delaying gratification will be simpler if you remind yourself of your objectives on a regular basis.

Be in the company of disciplined individuals.

To master self-discipline, you need to surround yourself with highly disciplined people. Be in the company of people who will help you reach your objectives. For example, if you're attempting to lose weight and avoid eating dessert, surround yourself with folks who have healthy eating habits.

Put long-term objectives first.

Your long-term objectives must always come before your present gratification. Never hesitate to remind yourself of your beliefs, ideals, and long-term goals when you feel like giving up.

Treat oneself.

Every time you are able to postpone satisfaction, treat yourself. This will make you more motivated to exercise self-control consistently.

Keep yourself well and get enough rest. The body can only process new habits if it is adequately nourished. You can experiment with the numbers to determine the ideal quantity. Once it is selected, follow through on it. Every night, try to go to bed and wake up at the same time. This will assist you in developing more self-control in your daily routine. There will be instances where plans do not work out. You can always correct your course and move past a few minor errors. They do occur.

Exercise is another beneficial habit to include in your everyday routine.

It takes regular exercise to keep the body in good condition. The word "exercise" has negative connotations for a lot of individuals. Physical activity need not be detrimental. This does not imply that you have to start training for a marathon or quit running to the gym. Whatever gets your body moving might be considered exercise. Get outside and play in the yard, walk, or jump rope with your kids. Enroll in a team. Think back to the good times you had playing baseball. Rake the leaves and tidy the garage.

Next, move the lawnmower around the area. Frequent movement helps to ease tension and stress.

Make every effort to plan. While some people are inherently structured, others must work very hard to develop their organizational skills. While failure is inevitable, the organization is not. Being organized requires work. Begin by putting one item in order. Take a drawer first. It's compact and simple to arrange. Ensure that you have a few boxes available. Examine the contents of the drawer and try to remember the last time you used each one. An object is no longer needed if it hasn't been utilized in six months. Make sure you have some boxes handy for when you work on this. If the item is in good shape, it can be donated. If it's no longer needed, it can be given to a good cause. Never hesitate to say no! Give anything that could be useful away.

It is best to safeguard it. After cleaning one drawer, go on to the next one. After organizing every drawer, proceed to the cabinets. As long as there are no extraneous items in the house, it will remain tidy and well-organized. It will become the norm to be clean.

Time management is another crucial objective for the development of discipline and good habits. Time management could be a managerial skill. If time is not managed efficiently, it will vanish, and all necessary activities will be unachievable. All that time management is is a strategy to bring structure and order to life. Organizing your tasks is a crucial aspect of time management. Eliminating unnecessary stuff from your cabinets and drawers can be an easy way to clean out the activities. The one needless task (constantly fixing the house) will end once the cabinets and drawers are tidy and orderly. It is that simple.

Think about all the time you lose each day on pointless pursuits. It's remarkable how much time it takes to find socks in laundry hampers when you can get them out of the drawer. Without a predetermined meal plan, how much time is lost trying to decide what to serve for supper? How much time are you squandering looking for the ideal pair of shoes? All of it adds up.

The secret to success in any discipline is perseverance. Giving up should never be the result of a brief setback. What keeps people going, even when things don't work out, is persistence. Failure is a necessary component of development. Finding an alternative to make things work is more important than doing something incorrectly. Rather than being a failure, it is a teaching moment.

Refusing to give up will make you more disciplined.

Don't let failure scare you. Only some achieve success on their first try. Actually, this is a positive thing. If self-control were effortless, it would be such. Trial and error is the process of personal progress. It is crucial to begin and give it a go. It won't work to talk about starting. A person who waits for the perfect moment to begin will never begin, even though it is wise to take some time to consider this new path. The terms "tomorrow," "someday," or "eventually," no longer belong in the lexicon of someone who wants self-discipline. This is it. The concepts in this book can assist you in selecting a goal. It doesn't have to, and shouldn't, be a major objective. Begin modestly. Smaller goals are easier to accomplish and have a higher chance of success than larger ones. Reaching a goal can provide you with a great sense of accomplishment and inspire you to take on more. Make a plan to do that. Set out to do the tasks necessary to achieve that objective.

You'll have to make the minor adjustments required to reach your objective. Give up negative behaviors. Resist temptation and embrace the new, healthy behaviors that will improve your living. You might stagger and fall. Fumble horribly. It will occur. If it does, don't give up. Get up, gather your strength, and shake off any dirt before you begin again. You may need to adjust the course of your road to success. The plan may have been flawed. It occurs. A perfect plan does not exist. Each strategy should be able to be updated as necessary. Keep your focus on the eventual goal. Remember that objective and make every effort to achieve it. Make a drawing and stick it on your fridge. Maintain a journal where you record every day's activities leading up to your objective. Inform your loved ones and friends about this objective. If something is obvious and conspicuous, it is simpler to forget. If it is not kept a secret, it will also be more difficult to ignore. Nobody desires to stumble in front of others! Anybody can use the knowledge in this book to become more disciplined. It will take some time, but it is achievable with commitment and focus.

Being Truthful to Yourself

One of the most crucial elements of self-discipline is being honest with yourself. You must understand who you are, what you are capable of, and what your role is. Perhaps you're fooling yourself into thinking things are going well in your relationship or work when they're not. It's likely that even while you're doing a wonderful job, you criticize yourself for not meeting your goals. In any case, having an honest conversation with oneself is a fantastic approach to developing life skills, overcoming obstacles, embracing oneself, and becoming more authentic. If you don't want to lose your capacity for self-control, you must be honest with yourself.

It's challenging to figure out how to be more honest with yourself. One of the hardest obstacles to overcome on the path to developing self-discipline maybe this one. These are the actions you can do to strengthen your self-discipline and, consequently, your self-honesty. You can prevent yourself from lying to yourself in this way. You don't need to persuade yourself to put off doing something. Rather, you have to work at realizing that you need to do a task. Be truthful with yourself about your aspirations and skills. The following actions will help you to be sincere with yourself. Observe these as much as is required.

First, assess yourself.

Choose a topic for introspection. This might be anything from your lover to your cleaning routine.

Show bravery. Choose a starting point that will offer you an advantage yet that you are confident you can achieve.

Allocate some time for your own needs. Give it your all to become the best version of yourself. Think. Consider everything in your basic material.

Put everything in writing. Respond to inquiries about yourself. Jot down your advantages and disadvantages. Consider the things that prevent you from succeeding. What is it that prevents you? What self-care actions are you taking? What is preventing you from moving forward and encouraging you to hold back?

Step 2: Go over and take action based on your self-evaluation.

Determine your areas of strength and need for improvement.

Never give up. Take action against these things that are impeding you.

Find out what your friends think of you. Invite your buddies to assist you.

Step 3: Track your development

Step 4: Revel in your accomplishments.

Regularly meditate

Coming from a former FBI and CIA agent, this may sound unusual, but meditation helps a lot with mental clarity and attention. These days, stress is one of the main causes for concern. When on field assignments and when operating secretly, I had to deal with high levels. There are a variety of meditation techniques available, such as Qi Gong, heart rhythm techniques, and transcendental meditation, which is the most popular kind I would have to use. Managing heart rate and central nervous system (which suppresses the "fight or flight" reaction) is essential for performing at your best under pressure. I go into greater detail about this in "Confidence: An Ex-Spy's Guide."

Aim to spend ten to fifteen minutes each day in meditation. The optimum time to meditate is in the morning. Take some time to unwind in the morning and avoid being rushed. After you get back from work, do the same and stop thinking about anything. This has always better equipped me for challenging and maybe difficult assignments.

booze and smoking

I don't mean to lecture you, but if you smoke or drink too much alcohol, for example, or if you have other unhealthy habits, you need to endeavor to reduce them. Clearly.

Spending patterns

You should also break the negative habit of extravagant spending. Create a saving routine and put safeguards in place to keep your spending within certain limits. You never know when this rainy-day savings will come in handy.

Partnerships

It will be crucial that you take note of the different relationships in your life. After all, in order to live fulfilling lives and contribute to society, all people require that the social aspects of our nature be met. When my parents were still living, this was more evident to me in my early adolescent and adult years. However, while the US government employed me, I also discovered that it was essential to establish and preserve positive, mutually beneficial relationships with both field accomplices and intelligence coworkers. These are some habits you should select to keep your relationships intact.

Discuss it.

Talking to your family and friends on a daily basis will be very beneficial. You will be able to stay in touch with them, even if it is only a small conversation. Please put in the time, and be sure you speak with them for at least ten minutes.

Pardoning

Many of us have a tendency to become enraged with friends or family too easily, which leads to pointless arguments. Tension and stress are the sole outcomes of this. Try to avoid engaging in any of these things and instead focus on forgiving and moving forward. Once you begin, others will take note and start doing the same.

Undoubtedly, adopting a forgiving mindset can improve your quality of life. It will help you manage problems like tension, rage, and hatred. These are all unnecessary feelings that must be addressed in the process of learning self-control. Try not to let your worries about who has harmed you consume your attention. Instead, concentrate on the essentials of life, like working toward your objectives. While cultivating such an attitude may seem difficult at first, doing so will only make it easier for you to remain disciplined.

Recall that when things appear out of your control, you can actually exert control over them by giving up control. Recognize the things you are powerless to alter, then take charge of them by choosing not to let them bring you any more grief.

Inspiration Identified

People frequently define motivation as the force that propels them to take action. This is what drives you to put in a lot of effort and strive toward your objectives. It significantly affects both your behavior and your capacity to accomplish your objectives.

There are several types of motivation, and each one affects how someone behaves. No one motivational strategy is effective for everyone. Since each person has a unique personality, so will their motivations.

Motivational Types

- Fear: This type of motivation is associated with repercussions and is typically employed when incentive motivation otherwise fails. This incentive may come in the form of penalties or unfavorable outcomes. This is frequently used to inspire students in educational settings, but it's also used to encourage staff members in professional contexts. You will receive some punishment for breaking the rules or failing to meet the objective.

- Incentive - This kind of motivation entails rewards, be they monetary or otherwise. Knowing they would receive anything when they accomplish a goal or target motivates a lot of people. Bonuses and promotions are excellent instances of this type of incentive.
- Growth: An internal motivator of sorts is the desire to better oneself. An intense desire to understand the outside world and yourself better can be a strong drive. People are naturally inclined to learn and develop. A person's desire for change can serve as motivation for personal development. , whether it be internal or external, or in their knowledge. It is believed that stagnation is both harmful and undesirable.
- Achievement: Also referred to as a drive for proficiency, accomplishment When you are driven to overcome obstacles and take on new challenges, you use motivators. It's when you want to develop your skills and prove to yourself and other people that you are

competent. This sense of success and accomplishment is, in general, something that is inherent.

- Social - A multitude of individuals are inspired by diverse social factors. It may stem from a desire to fit in or be accepted by a particular peer group, or it may stem from a desire to make new friends locally or globally. You are driven by an innate need for acceptance and affiliation, as well as a need to feel a sense of community. A strong and sincere desire to improve and make a difference in the lives of others is another form of social motivation. Social issues are almost certainly what drive you to want to change the world.
- Power: Motivation for power can manifest as a desire for autonomy or control over others. You desire autonomy over your life and the ability to make choices for yourself. You desire for the capacity to govern the way you live now and how your life will unfold in the future. Furthermore, some people desire to impose control over those

around them. Some people have a stronger yearning for this than the rest of us. In some cases, this desire for power can lead to immoral, unlawful, or destructive actions. In other cases, the desire for power is as simple as the desire to influence the actions of others. It is when you want people to do what you want according to your schedule and how you want things

Apply The Rollover Technique

It can be challenging to adopt a new lifestyle, particularly one that requires more self-discipline and is likely to differ greatly from your previous way of living. This is the reason you shouldn't try to do too much too quickly while making your list of how you want to spend your time. To help you settle into your new routine, set yourself a few easy activities to begin with. Feel free to add more items to the mix once you've been using them for a few weeks and are comfortable with the quantity.

As an additional note, however, if you do not manage to complete all of your activities in a given week—for example, you met all of your written tasks but never got around to building that bookshelf—be sure to carry over that item to the next week when you create your to-do list. This guarantees that anything you put down will finally be completed. It would also be prudent to maintain a consistent number of items on your weekly to-do list and refrain from adding new things until you have completed the previous week's tasks. This keeps you from becoming overwhelmed by the amount of stuff you were unable to finish in the last weeks.

Learn the Essentials

To develop self-discipline, you must first grasp the fundamentals. Let us begin:

Rest.

You might be wondering why we would begin a book on self-discipline with something as unimportant as sleep. Your willpower is impacted by the quality of your sleep, which is the reason. This review demonstrates that will and the quality of your sleep are strongly correlated. According to this study, employees who don't get enough sleep are more prone to act on impulse, make poor decisions, and find it difficult to concentrate at work. Your ability to practice self-control is diminished by irregular sleep patterns, which also lessen the energy required for self-control. The quality of your nightly sleep has an impact on your level of productivity at work. Research has shown that sleep issues impact the synthesis of hormones and neurotransmitters. This leads to disturbances in the management of emotions and regular thinking processes. REM (rapid eye movement) during sleep improves memory and learning, according to other studies.

Here are a few helpful pointers for restful sleep

Set a consistent bedtime: Establish a regular bedtime; select a time when you feel drowsy and exhausted most of the time. Even on the weekends, stick to the schedule. If you must adjust your bedtime, do so gradually—by ten to fifteen minutes each way.

Make an effort to wake up daily at the same time: You should not need an alarm clock to wake up at the same time every day if you get seven to eight hours of sleep every night. The simple explanation for needing an alarm clock to wake up is insufficient sleep.

Take a nap during the day to make up for lost sleep if you don't get enough at night. This is preferable to staying up late to sleep. If you have insomnia, you need to be cautious when taking naps. Sleeping worsens insomnia.

Avoid sleeping before bed: If you start to feel drowsy after supper, try doing something moderately stimulating, like taking a stroll or doing the dishes. However, avoid sleeping before bedtime.

Before going to bed, turn off the TV and computer. Avoid watching TV right before bed. A few people watch TV right before going to bed as a habit. In actuality, this interferes with falling asleep. Instead, turn on some relaxing music.

Avoid reading on an iPad or other backlit gadget right before bed. Use an e-reader if reading is required of you.

When attempting to fall asleep, make sure your bedroom is dark and reserve it solely for sleeping and having sex.

Maintain a cool room. About 18°C is ideal.

Verify that the bed is cozy. This typically refers to a premium firm mattress that supports the spine and prevents the body from remaining in the middle of the bed.

Avoid using gadgets with backlights, like iPads, right before bed. When reading, use an e-reader.

Just go to bed for sex and sleep. Before you go to bed, make your bedroom cold and dark.

When you sleep, make sure your mattress is comfy.

Avoid consuming a large meal right before bed. Eating large meals right before bed hinders digestion, which makes you feel bad and clumsy during the day.

Avoid coffee and smoking at least three hours before bed, and don't drink alcohol right before bed.

What Exactly Is Self-Discipline Anyway?

Although there are numerous definitions of self-discipline, I like the American writer and philosopher Elbert Hubbard's description the best. According to him, self-discipline is "the ability to do what needs to be done, whether you feel like it or not," at the appropriate time.

One vital life skill that enables you to succeed in anything you want to pursue is self-discipline. Once more, money is not necessarily a factor in this. These can involve the relationships you have. This may also impact your health.

If you're like most Americans, you undoubtedly already know that losing weight is no joke. It requires an incredible amount of self-control because, if given the chance, we'd much prefer to eat pizza. We'd like to have some fried chicken or a burger.

However, it takes a great deal of self-control to eat a salad every day.

Δ

Self-Control Lets You Concentrate.

Being disciplined teaches you to remember what your top priorities are. You choose your preferences and set daily goals based on what matters most.

After you've completed it, your self-control comes into play, and you can concentrate on it every day. Your words, deeds, and ideas all work toward that end.

You do a lot of other things, of course, but your life has a recurring theme. This persistent focus is present. It's more complex than chasing your tail or circling the wagons.

You're getting closer to that huge goal; therefore, that's why your day has significance. Training is required for this. It also requires the capacity to turn down quick fixes and superficial temptations.

There are numerous examples. As a matter of fact, their numbers are excessive. Every step you take and every day you spend brings you closer to the intended result when you choose to keep your eyes on the big picture and take care of the things that need to be taken care of.

This does not mean that you will go any quicker. This means that everything will go differently than planned and that your path will be simple.

In actuality, unforeseen difficulties are nearly always present when pursuing a major objective. Life is constantly giving you curve balls.

Disciplined people, on the other hand, discover within themselves the ability to resolve issues and overcome obstacles when they come up. You remain conscious. You are not coerced into quitting. They don't take away your resolve.

None of those things are what they do. Rather, you discover the inner strength to keep moving on and aim for the end goal of success. That is restraint.

It's not overly dramatic or seductive. This movie isn't this one. It's not like there aren't any surprises, thrills, or spills along the route or like there's a conspiracy of individuals working against you. Nope.

Generally speaking, practicing self-discipline on a daily basis means doing the same thing. It is tedious. It is unrelated to sexual activity.

But every step you take changes who you are. As you withstand temptation after temptation, your strength grows.

Eventually, you'll find yourself asking yourself, "What am I thinking? There are a lot of other easy things I can accomplish. I could have always gone in many directions. What am I considering?

You have to figure out the "why." Put otherwise, you need to decide what your aim is. If not, moving forward will be challenging.

Self-control allows you to concentrate.

Being self-disciplined teaches you how to maintain your attention on your top priorities. You make decisions about your objectives and daily priorities based on what matters most.

Your self-control will then start to take over, and you will be able to focus on it every single day. Your words, ideas, and deeds all work toward achieving that objective.

You're engaged in a lot of other activities, of course, but one aspect of your life keeps coming up. This constant focus is present. It's not as simple as chasing your tail or spinning your wheels.

There comes a time in the day when you know that you're getting closer to that big achievement in the back of your mind. It takes training for this. It also calls for the capacity to resist quick fixes and superficial temptations.

Those are in great plenty. Far too many exist. Whenever you opt to concentrate on the bigger picture and attend to the things that require your attention, each day that passes and each action you do will bring you one step closer to achieving your goal.

This does not, however, imply that your trip will go more quickly. This doesn't mean that everything will be simple or that your journey will go well.

There are virtually always obstacles you weren't prepared for when pursuing a major objective. Life is sending you curveball after curveball.

Interestingly enough, though, when you practice discipline, you discover that you have what it takes to overcome obstacles and find solutions to issues as they arise. Nothing knocks you out. They don't force you to give up. They don't sap your willpower.

They do none of that. Instead, you discover that you have what it takes to keep moving forward in the direction of that final triumph. That is self-control.

It's not overly dramatic or seductive. The movies are not this. It's not like there's a vast conspiracy of people working against you, and the journey is full of surprises, thrills, and spills. Nope.

Generally speaking, practicing self-discipline on a daily basis entails doing the same thing repeatedly. It's laborious. It's not in the slightest bit seductive.

But every step you take is altering your character. Refusing temptation after temptation makes you stronger and stronger.

You will eventually come to ask yourself, "Why am I doing this? I can do so many other things that are much simpler. Other shortcuts are always an option that I could have explored. I'm doing this, but why?"

Quit Putting Things Off

Like other actions and behaviors, procrastination is a habit that develops into a natural way of being for us after prolonged use. Procrastinators, for example, will always find a method to undermine themselves in order to prolong their delays. They will always come up with excuses for why they are running behind schedule. There are explanations for why people choose to put things off. Fear is the main cause of people's procrastination and justifications for why they fall short of their objectives. When someone says, "I can't help it," that is their justification; instead of taking responsibility for their actions and moving on to complain about things that are not happening in their lives, they would much rather sit with their excuse. Many people have the desire to start their own business and have this concept in their head, but they come up with an excuse like they need more money to get started or that they need to save some cash first. Well, guess what? These may seem like reasonable justifications, but if you notice it becomes a habit or a pattern that you can't break, it ends up becoming the reason why individuals wind up postponing instead of acting.

The main cause of procrastination has been people's fear of failing or being mocked. Knowing a business is more crucial to an entrepreneur than having money invested in it. You will lose money to get experience if you don't go through the learning process, and in the business world, it's said that you have learned the hard way. Offering services and searching for opportunities and gaps that others need to perceive are the cornerstones of entrepreneurship. If you can close such gaps and provide a service, you will draw in business.

You must give up waiting for everything to get perfect since it will never be perfect, and the conditions will never be ideal if you want to achieve success, wealth, or your aspirations. Many people's aspirations have been dashed and postponed because they become chronic procrastinators, constantly waiting for the perfect opportunity, while in the meantime, someone else is living out the dream you desire for yourself despite your lack of organization. I promise you that if you procrastinate, it will kill your concept and take away your destiny because the only positive outcomes are mediocrity and stagnation. The good news is that you can be someone other than an expert to get started. As we move forward, destiny has a way of bringing people into our lives to make up for any gaps in any one area. Suppose you decide that you want to go forward and will no longer put things off. There are so many successes waiting for you to achieve them, but by procrastinating, you will not have access to them. You may feel as though you don't have everything you need, but don't worry—the people you need will be drawn to you for the action you are taking. Here are some pointers to help you stop putting things off.

Start by making a plan. Next, draft a backup plan. Any program that has a fallback in place is better than none at all. A significant element of weight loss will be adopting healthy eating habits. At home, where you have total control over the menu, this is simple to accomplish. When you get the invitation to the party, what happens? Connecting with friends and family over a well-planned party is a terrific idea. And the food, all of it? This is the backup plan. You have a fallback strategy in place to eat less already. The idea is to sample everything with one mouthful and then mingle with other guests for the remainder of the evening. The second plan is this one. This will guarantee that the aim is maintained and aid in maintaining the original plan in place.

When the aim is accomplished, remember to reward them with a treat. Rewarding good behavior is what makes people happy. Select a reward that fits the objective. You can give up smoking in your home and paint the walls. Your home will smell wonderful and look fantastic. If the vehicle has yet to be smoked in, it is worthwhile to get it detailed. A brand-new automobile has an amazing scent. If your weight loss goals have been met, treat yourself to a new wardrobe.

Recognize that mistakes will happen occasionally. It doesn't imply that you ought to aim for failure. This entails accepting defeat as it occurs. People are people. It will not work. Though they will occasionally fail, they will attempt. Acknowledge that loss is unavoidable. Recognize your failure. Avoid feeling resentful or guilty. These feelings are common and might get in the way of your goal-achieving efforts. Take lessons from your errors. How did it turn out? What took place? What steps may be taken to ensure that this does not occur again? Failure can be overcome if it has been recognized and examined. You are still headed in the correct direction. It might require some adjusting. There may have to be a small bend. Regaining your focus is the first step toward accomplishing any goal. Additionally, this is the beginning of self-discipline.

Comprehending Self-Control

Self-discipline: what is it? It's the capacity to refuse cake when you're trying to lose weight and you've had enough. It is the capacity to awaken on schedule. It's the capacity to work and avoid consuming social media for the majority of your time. It's the capacity to refuse a second drink when you realize you've had enough. It is crucial to understand that self-control manifests itself in a variety of ways. These comprise: -The capacity to endure adversity and the fortitude to move forward in the face of obstacles and disappointments.

-The ability to stay focused and avoid getting sidetracked; -The strength to withstand temptation; -The fervor to break negative habits; -The drive to achieve your goals; -The determination to keep trying until you succeed

Being self-disciplined will put you in a wonderful position to concentrate on reaching your objectives. The most important thing to keep in mind is that discipline is a talent. It must, therefore, be regularly practiced and developed, just like any other ability.

We will examine methods for developing self-control and self-discipline in the upcoming chapters.

Boost Your Will Power

The unique quality that gives you the ability to control or positively impact your own will is known as willpower. You can withstand negative impulses and maintain an informed decision by using your willpower.

A strong weapon that can help you take control of your life and improve your self-discipline is willpower. But prudence is advisable. You should be aware that your will varies based on the conditions and time of day. Your willpower typically wanes when you are worn out and under stress. You are less likely to follow your healthy eating plan and more inclined to order takeout after a "difficult" day. Being "too tired" to play with your child makes you, as a parent, more likely to let him watch TV. Looking at your workout schedule increases the likelihood that you'll get in bed and decide to "do extra push-ups tomorrow."

It would be best if you made an effort to fortify your willpower because of this. Strengthening your resolve will enable you to persevere and achieve your goals in the face of unfavorable situations.

Let's examine how you can accomplish this:

Increasing your pressure threshold

As said previously, there may be occasions when you give in to your urges due to external factors. You can, however, get around this by strengthening your pressure tolerance. Little things like listening to your inner voice and delaying doing anything till the next day are where it all begins. There are always other tomorrows, as the proverb "tomorrow never comes" suggests. If you keep putting off the things you need to accomplish, you might need help to do them. The dishes you put off doing tonight will be there when you wake up. Give up delaying.

Could you not put off doing it? You will be able to strengthen your willpower gradually. You've also improved your ability to handle pressure, so even in situations where you have to make tough choices, you will be able to apply your willpower.

The Five Distractions from Self-Control

Paulo's made-up story establishes the mood for the rest of our voyage and provides you with the instructions to drive your car rather than delegating control to someone else. It's occasionally useful to let someone else go, but it's only a coincidence that they are heading to the same place you might want to visit, or even that they are taking the same road past a lake or forest you might want to explore.

Me and my discipline

I want to offer a quick overview of my life before delving deeply into self-control, focusing on how I became entangled in compulsions. The good news is that I made it through by using conscious self-control.

Until I decided to give my shoulders a break and let go of the ten years' worth of obsessive behavior, I carried around a different version of myself. Following a childhood experience in which my father and grandmother both passed away in less than a month, something slowly started to change in the deepest recess of my memory. The awareness of being joyful and alive was vanishing like smoke from a fire that devoured entities that were alive only a second before.

I never asked my parents to buy me anything when I was a child. I'd never felt the need to smoke or drink, but once my father passed away, I don't know what changed, but all of a sudden, I started to desire material things. Power, money, booze, and other things that had never occurred to me before became things I sought.

These addictions started to occur on a daily basis in my life. And as they always do, the clouds gradually and methodically seized control of the world I had made for myself. I was identified as having clinical anxiety and depression. The darkest storms I had ever experienced swept me away just when my family needed me the most. I felt like there was a huge hole in my life, and I apologized for not being there for them.

In an attempt to get over these emotions, I ate and bought everything I could get my hands on, gave in to my need to overindulge in alcohol and cigarettes, obsessively thought things out, and entered into failed relationships. Looking back now, I am really grateful that I was made aware of the conscious being that lives inside every one of us.

One day, a colleague took me to an ashram in South India to sign up for a yoga and meditation camp after I had lived ten years of unjustified ignorance. I went there because I didn't have much to do that weekend, and the center was planned and only around a hundred km on the outskirts of the city. I just packed my car with food and drink and headed to the camp. My pal was in there, working nonstop, checking inventory, and organizing visitor passes, among other things.

I was thinking how foolish it was of him to labor for someone else unpaid. At that point, the Satsang (event) got underway, and a monk began to talk in a deep voice. Something jolted me from inside; I could feel the vibration in me. He spoke about the importance of impermanence and how we build our own social and security networks, which ultimately engulf us.

I was so enthralled that I requested time off from work and volunteered at the ashram. I gained knowledge of self-control, mindfulness, and how to accomplish goals without criticizing myself. I organized multiple nonprofit yoga and meditation programs in India and started practicing Maha-mudra meditation on a daily basis. I understood that even after performing yoga and meditation, my anxiety and compulsiveness did not evaporate altogether, but it did help me live with it better.

Signs And Symptoms

A mind that won't seem to shut off can be one of the most painful and demanding ordeals to live with. Could you imagine never having a break from your constant negative thoughts? Well, if you're an overthinker (or suspect you might be), you probably have an intuition about what that feels like already. In your darkest and most terrible moments, it can feel like you're all alone in this world, but it is crucial to realize that you're not.

You could ask yourself: Why is overthinking such a negative thing if I'm spending extra time attempting to come up with a master plan? At some time, we've all encountered those situations where we think: If only I had done what

I was supposed to do in the first place. That's one of the many drawbacks of this poor behavior. It leads to a false sense of security and the idea that you're making progress when, in reality, you're spending too much time preparing and thinking about the actions that should be taken. You end up losing the opportunity to act entirely. Let's investigate this in greater detail.

How to Identify If You're an Overthinker

If given a choice, no one would choose to live with a broken record in their head. No one wants to contemplate the same negative notion continuously till they feel like they're perhaps going nuts. Since the mind is where it all begins, if you don't have peace in your thoughts, you don't have peace of mind. How do you determine whether your mind is holding back? Well, the first thing to do is to identify if you're an overthinker.

Getting to the base of the problem entails having the ability to accept that there is a problem to begin with.

You might be an overthinker if you relate to any of the indicators below that indicate your thoughts are the ones controlling the show:

• Confusion - If you discover you're trying to retain a clear head, you're likely thinking too much, and that's producing the confusion that you experience. You repeat things that you've stated several times before; you exhibit some obsessive-compulsive behaviors like routinely repeating actions or routines since you can't recall if you've done them already. You seek confirmation regarding the same item multiple times but still have a feeling of unpleasant doubt. Without the ability to regulate your emotions and your ideas, your mind can quickly get carried away, and when it happens, confusion swiftly follows.

- Consistent Negative Perception - You always perceive the negative in everything that happens. A mind that is swamped with thoughts continuously struggles to see the silver lining, even if it's right there in front of you. Overthinkers tend to jump toward the bad automatically, and the mind grabs onto that, unwilling to let go.

- Self-Doubt - Overthinkers don't trust their judgment. That's partly because they struggle with perfectionism, which is unreasonable. When they fall short, they feel incompetent and lose confidence in their talents. Self-doubt can be a terrible load to bear, and as soon it gains a stronghold in your head, it can be a very tough habit to break out of. We know that we shouldn't focus on the negative. We are aware that self-belief is important.

• Often Feeling Exhausted: Thinking negatively saps your vitality. When you combine that with overthinking, which may cause your mind to race a mile a minute, it makes sense that even after obtaining the necessary rest, you still feel worn out and unmotivated. Even when you haven't done much, you feel worn out. You start to feel lazy, move slowly, and everything seems like it would take a lot of work to finish. That's probably because, even though you should be sleeping, when you think too much, your mind never truly stops.

• Your Life Is Ruled by Fear - Now that it has been shown that fear is the root cause of a large portion of overthinking, living a life controlled by fear is another telltale indicator that you are an overthinker. You no longer feel free to enjoy life and feel stuck. Even before you leave the house every day, there appears to be something to be concerned about. Fear is a natural human emotion. Fear has become an ingrained aspect of the lives of overthinkers. You may be an overthinker yourself if your fear has gotten to the point that it prevents you from living your life and pursuing your goals.

• Afraid of Failure - To become good at anything, you need to be comfortable with the concept of failing. But this is something an overthinker cannot achieve since they're frightened of failure. You didn't find learning to walk frightening as a toddler. It made no difference how many times you stumbled and what transpired on each try. You persisted in trying until you eventually mastered walking. You never considered giving up at this point. Clearly, avoiding failure is something we learned to develop later in life. Most of us grow terrified of failing and embarrassing ourselves, and for an overthinker, this dread is compounded. They become stagnant as a result, and if you see that this is the case for you, you may be more powerful than you realize with your thoughts.

• Overanalyzing – While thinking too much might cause anxiety, overanalyzing can also cause it. This kind of behavior is typical of overthinkers because they are easily distracted by their ideas and strive for impractical perfection. They attempt to make everything as flawless as possible before deciding to take any form of action.

Since perfection is not a totally attainable notion all the time, overthinkers find themselves in the paralysis-by-analysis state that was mentioned in The Plan, plan, and Plan some more, but that's about it.

- Unrealistic Deadlines: Overthinkers may be the ones setting these deadlines themselves, or they may be working for an employer who does. Unrealistic deadlines sometimes cause stress, and when you push yourself too hard too quickly, you become overwhelmed and give in to the influence of your negative thoughts. Overthinkers occasionally take on more than they can manage out of concern of being viewed unfavorably due to the dread of failure they live with. They wish to avoid having the perception that they are unworthy or inept. However, if you're an overthinker who places unreasonable expectations on yourself, setting excessive standards will not help you escape the cycle of tension and negative thought patterns.

Do The Right People Not Require Inspiration?

Jim Collins, a global authority in family business management, once stated "you don't need to worry about motivating them if you have the right people on your bus." My friend said, "Does this mean that employee motivation programs are useless?" If we could only perfect our hiring process, we could hire a large number of self-starters who wouldn't require management encouragement. Whoa, might that save costs? Yep. Thus, this seems like a good idea—no, a fantastic idea—but is it?

There is truth to what Jim Collins says, but he isn't entirely correct.

First things first, we must return the problem to a familiar place. The majority of hiring decisions are made based on credentials and experience; frequently, this means that high energy—which is effectively strong motivation—is the most important factor in outperformance. Thus, it makes sense to approach and recruit these individuals in the first instance, but how should we go about doing that? It is difficult to determine in the first instance which types of people are generally motivated; however, we do know that the majority of interview subjects seem motivated and that performing exceptionally well in interviews typically indicates that a candidate is excellent during the interview rather than being excellent for the position for which they are being interviewed!

After you've got these people, though, the idea that they won't stop being motivated if you don't do anything for them is unrealistic. Sure, like the Duracell bunny, they'll run farther and faster than the unmotivated people you first brought in, but they still require effort—less effort than the unmotivated people, but effort nonetheless. Even though it could be argued that highly effective people are self-starters, the benefit of inputs is also related to reading their minds; if you don't put anything down, you're not likely to really discover what's going on inside their head, and boom, the self-starter up and leaves because there's no interaction with them.

Thus, it is imperative to provide the most motivated with even more motivation; this leads to the phenomenon of reciprocation; after all, the most exceptional people naturally strive to be better; thus, assisting them genuinely elevates you to the highest levels of performance while, concurrently, increasing buy-in and retention rates in the relationship.

The fact is—the obvious truth is—that things change, especially motivation. We are all aware of highly motivated, accomplished men and women who were once outsiders but have since fallen by the wayside and become, occasionally, positive liabilities. What transpired with them? Many things can happen to them: they may burn out over one thing, neglect another, or lack meaning or purpose. In any case, why am I doing this when I never see my family again?

Thus, you should hire highly motivated people—that's wise counsel from Jim Collins. Don't imagine the task done, though! Similar to physical fitness, maintaining motivation requires consistent and persistent effort, no matter where you are in life. Those who are self-motivated may indeed do a lot for themselves, but let's be clear: Management has a lot to offer to maintain exceptionally high performance.

The issue around motivation.

Motivation means taking action and reading about exercise means staying in shape. Both are possible, of course, but motivation alone accomplishes nothing, even while it appears to be accomplishing something.

Motivation is never the issue. Look at January 1st for everyone at all. Everybody is excited to start making changes in the new year. Not that we don't want to do things, our issue is that the majority of us never follow through.

I'm not going to write a single word just because I'm motivated to write articles. Just because I'm motivated to eat less vegan chocolates, that doesn't mean I will. Motivation seems significant because it seems like action, even though it isn't.

We try to motivate ourselves by imagining how much better our lives will be after we are motivated, or by getting enthusiastic about future possibilities. The problem isn't that we want something; rather, it's that we believe our desire for something makes us more likely to get it.

Motivation is theoretical, even for mundane tasks like exercising or writing more wherever action is tangible.

We lose ourselves when our idealized ideas of wanting something to happen proceed farther and farther from really putting it into practice. We give up and frequently act oppositely (for example, "It doesn't matter if I have junk food for dinner because I didn't have a healthy lunch today" or "Why write anything now? I ought should have been writing for the past two weeks and completed 10,000 words by now."

The problem with motivation is that we need more motivation. Instead of just working, we imagine that we need to be motivated in the first place. In the case of creativity, in particular, it's simple to fall into the mindset of waiting for inspiration. Still, the greatest way for the inspiration to visit us is actually to go to work.

Ultimately, motivation is insignificant; action is what matters because it is the activity that generates the work.

Discipline is necessary for action; therefore we tell our minds to shut up. We must cease telling ourselves to be motivated or feel defeated when we fail to act on our motivation sooner. We cannot debate with ourselves since, even in the end, we always lose.

Self-Discipline Habit

We've seen that one of the biggest obstacles to success is a lack of self-control. Enhancing your self-control will significantly boost your chances of success, and you can achieve this by cultivating the subsequent behaviors:

Put Your Energy Into Something You Are Passionate About

Self-discipline will come easily if you are passionate about what you do. As we've seen, exercising self-discipline means concentrating on your main responsibilities and resisting the need to do what is now comfortable. It becomes an uphill battle to pursue something you are not passionate about. On the other hand, choosing an activity you enjoy will make it much simpler for you to avoid putting things off.

Eliminate Any Possible Diversions

Self-disciplined people typically eliminate possible distractions from their surroundings. Avoiding distractions that could divert your attention from the important tasks at hand is the foundation of self-discipline. Distractions might be avoided altogether rather than placing yourself in a situation where you have to battle them continuously. For instance, you can turn off all of your emails, messages, and social media notifications if you need to focus on a project or study for the next six hours. If you don't need the internet for work, you can even turn it off. If your phone is buzzing with notifications every other minute, you will need more time to concentrate on your task.

Prioritize the hardest tasks first.

Because the tasks we are performing on projects can vary in difficulty, we frequently find ourselves stuck. That means that if you are doing easy chores and then come across a challenging one, there's a good risk you'll stop or lose attention. Doing the most difficult tasks first will help you maintain discipline. Examine your project as a whole to determine which tasks are the most involved, then arrange your workflow such that those jobs are completed first. After completing the challenging tasks, things get easier.

Make Quick Choices

One of the biggest causes of people's inability to concentrate on their tasks and maintain self-discipline is indecision. Occasionally, we squander time acquiring "more information" rather than taking action. You must operate from the idea that "done is better than perfect" if you want to make judgments quickly. Rather than wasting time trying to figure out how to do anything properly, it is preferable to get whatever you have to accomplish done. The reason for this is because overabundance of knowledge causes "decision paralysis," and perfection is an illusion.

Developing Positive Habits Promotes Positive Self-Discipline

It takes time to form excellent habits, but since they are the cornerstones of developing self-control, I can guarantee that the time you invest in doing so will be well spent.

Habits are routine behaviors or acts that you perform automatically or repeatedly. You start doing it without thinking since it's become so ingrained in your everyday routine, and you're so accustomed to it. Your habit is something you do without even thinking about it beforehand.

Discipline is not a cage; it is freedom.

Whenever I discuss self-discipline with individuals, I frequently need clarification. People think that order, productivity, discipline, and structure equate to boredom. They compare everything to a cage of some sort. They feel that discipline is a set of rules and restrictions that they are unable to cross, even though they truly want to. Put, the jail.

And I'll tell you a story before I give you my thoughts on these matters. Bees were flying over their hive on a bright day. Emma is one bee in particular that deserves our attention. Emma is doing great; she can fly and has no fear. Like any other typical bee, she goes out and gathers pollen, socializes with her friends and girlfriends, and overall has a fantastic time. Emma has aspirations and objectives in life that she hopes to fulfill. She envisions what lies ahead of her, anticipates her lengthy life, and so forth. Suddenly, though, a bear appears close to the hive. The bear is ready to take the honey because it is hungry. As the bear approaches, Emma's instinct takes over and she leaps at him, stinging him between the eyes. Emma finds herself stuck when she tries to fly away due to the bear's incredibly thick skin. Yes, in order to fly away, she must now give up her sting. This is what occurs, but regrettably, bees cannot survive without their sting; otherwise, they would perish very soon. Emma had no option, which is the saddest part of this situation. In order to defend their home, bees have evolved a self-destructive tendency throughout millions of years of evolutionary growth. As a result, Emma fought the bear out of pure instinct and perished. Stated differently, her destiny was set. She would have likely flown far away to fulfill her hopes and goals if she had known that things would end this way. The bee is unconscious and unable to regulate its behavior. Furthermore, she is not to fault for making such a stupid choice. Her own nature has imprisoned her.

Now, let us return to the question of freedom. I find it hard to understand when people refer to self-control as a jail. Is a biological jail preferable? Is giving in to your animal instincts truly preferable to living a life on your own terms? A man, after all, is not limited by his animal instincts like bees are. Nature has bestowed upon us the capacity for free will. Should we possess such a capability, we ought to employ it. Why are we even human if we don't use it? Being born into a bee species that lacks self-control was worth it.

Your desire may be to write a book, attain a professional objective, follow a healthy diet, or get in better physical shape. We have a deep desire for this to occur and have particular dreams for our lives. Additionally, there is a specific bridge that connects our current location to the destination. a bridge spanning a vast chasm. We discover a plethora of fleeting delights on this bridge, all of which so allure us. However, our chances of achieving the ultimate objective decrease as we play on the bridge more. Fortunately, we are more disciplined than bees. If we walk across a wide bridge without getting sidetracked by anything, we can overcome fleeting instincts. It is self-discipline that enables us to accomplish our most important goals. Unlike bees, we do not have to risk our lives to attack the bear. So how, given our logic, can discipline be compared to a prison?

If you stop to think about it, we are all in prison regardless; we are just in a conscious prison when it comes to self-discipline. This is the kind of prison that suits our personal interests. It appears more liberated. And in the absence of self-discipline, this is a prison of external conditions that do not care about our interests.

That is why an undisciplined person renounces freedom for the dubious pleasure of being locked in the prison of his own instincts.

Of course, our modern capitalist world knows how much we love novelty and pleasure. Therefore, it bombards us with the strongest incentives in the name of profit. However, there is some good news. It consists of the fact that no matter how much the world around us and our animal heritage press us, we can break free from prison. Into a new world of self-discipline, order of awareness, and organization. We have a choice to be free.

Getting Things Done: The Significance Of Self-Determination And Good-Habit Information

Let me begin with a story. My family member recently left the dishwasher door open for no apparent reason. I came strolling along, and because of the baking pan that I was holding, which was blocking my view (and also because I wasn't expecting someone to leave the door down for any appropriate reason), I didn't realize that the door was actually down. My hair slipped to the edge, and the baking pan and I almost toppled over the extended dish rack. The circumstances demanded an intervention, I used one.

After some time had passed and the agony had subsided (unfortunately, not before the swelling and bruises had), I felt that this would be a good opportunity to remind the family member that homeowners have guidelines like "If you open it, close it" for sensible, common sense reasons. For all of the residents of the home, they assist in forming the foundation of a considerate, courteous, and, in this case, much safer atmosphere.

The keys to successfully implementing this specific design-based blueprint, as well as many others similar to it, are as follows: "If you turn it on, turn it off." "If you take something out, store it away," and all the others are about developing positive habits and self-control.

Notably, however, self-discipline and good-habit communication are two essential components of organizational success! (You sucked that clogging.)

Therefore, they are essential in the sense that they constitute the fifth of what I refer to as the "five foundations of organization":

1. Capacity This means that an individual does not possess—or is unable to accommodate—conditions like chronic illness, psychiatric disorders, grief, depression, OCD, chronic fatigue syndrome, ADD/ADHD, PTSD, hoarding, and other behaviors, circumstances, or conditions that impair an individual's ability to be more organized. They don't need to be depressed because help is available for all of these circumstances; yet, without it, they may experience unusual accelerations in their efforts to become more structured.

2. WillĖngness: You are unable to force someone to perform any action. People have to be open to change.

3. Dedication: Ability and willingness are excellent beginnings, but they need to be supported by a dedication of time and

energy to the organizational procedures and the implementation of constructive changes. Good intentions are insufficient.

4. Tools: These can be tangible items like hooks, shelves, and storage tubs, or they can be procedures and systems that make people more productive and efficient. In this way, the fourth fundamental is the starting point where a friend, family member, or professional organizer can introduce the process to assist someone in becoming more organized, as the preceding three must already be present in order to make progress. (This is the traditional three-legged stool analogy: the stool will become stronger with the addition of more legs, but the first three must be there for the seat to stand.)

5. Routines: Hey, look at them! As an organizer, I have assisted clients in

getting rid of items they no longer need, use, or love. I have helped them in returning the "keepers" in a more organized and efficient manner. We have been "confined" until we have become purple. We have created processes and systems that mesh with the ways in which they live, work, and think. We also discussed how to keep everything organized, light, and spacious that we have created.

However, that's where the unleast clients' self-discipline and good-habit formation begins. The first four fundamentals will organize them, but only the last one will maintain their organization because it's an inconvenient truth (to borrow a phrase) that the criminal never fails to reappear. Through their hard effort, organizers and other healthcare professionals can raise their chances of success, but they are unable to provide customers with that final crucial component. But what they can do is remind them that what's left of their new, healthy habits will gain momentum, which will reinforce their positive behavior and inspire them to keep up the good work.

Tenacity And Self-Control

"Avoid trying to become a great man in a hurry. One in ten thousand possibilities of success

The exercise of self-control involves persistence. The ability to keep going in the face of obstacles and short-term failures is necessary for success in life. Self-esteem and perseverance are related in that each time you push yourself to keep going, you feel better about yourself. You'll feel better about yourself and have more self-assurance. Perseverance can be aided by optimism or having faith in your ability to succeed in the long run. See the good in every situation and the valuable lesson in every setback.

How many times you get knocked down in life doesn't matter. The number of times you get back up after falling is more important than how many times you fall. You will eventually succeed if you keep getting back up.

Chapter 8: Tasks and Individual Control

For top leaders, the two most important abilities to have at work are:

The capacity to work on high-value initiatives and prioritize duties

the commitment to do a task quickly and effectively.

About half of an employee's time is spent on "non-work related" activities, such as chit-chatting with coworkers, taking long lunch and coffee breaks, using the internet, reading the newspaper, and other such activities. According to Brian Tracy, it's imperative to distinguish between what is important and irrelevant information. The Pareto principle can be applied in this case: Eighty percent of your work is accounted for by twenty percent of your tasks. Identifying such tasks and concentrating on doing them properly is your aim.

Setting priorities is a goal that you can accomplish with the help of the Law of Three. The process basically consists of making a list of everything you do Monday through Friday of a workweek and then asking yourself, "What are the three things/activities/tasks that add the most value to the company?" These three main factors should account for about 80–90% of the company's value. It is your responsibility to recognize them and then set aside time each day to finish them.

People will constantly make an effort to divert you from your most vital tasks. A lot of the time, they waste their own time. Could you make an effort to avoid them? The goal is to put in a lot of action throughout your entire shift. This calls for a lot of self-control since you have to keep pushing beyond interruptions and distractions in order to focus on the crucial task at hand, which is your work. There is a straightforward three-part formula for success in the workplace: arrive a little early, work a little harder, and stay a little later.

Chapter 1 explains the meaning of self-discipline and its significance.

The capacity to exercise self-control and self-motivation to make the proper decisions is known as self-discipline. Say, for example, that you are working and at your wits' end when you spill your coffee on your laptop, and now you are going to lose it. Lack of self-discipline increases the likelihood of irrational thinking, rash decisions, and worsening of the circumstances. Let's now envision a disciplined situation. After spilling coffee, this individual acts logically, making amends and soothing themselves by going for a walk outside and other such activities.

Willpower is necessary to think clearly in such circumstances and behave logically, yet willpower is a finite resource. However, with proper use, it can be increased with time. Consider it like a muscle: the more you properly exercise it, the stronger and more developed it becomes. For the time being, let's set it aside; we'll learn more about it in the coming chapters.

That's just an oversimplified interpretation of what self-control actually entails. As it happens, it has a profound effect on you that changes your life in ways you can't even begin to comprehend. You possess the capacity to inspire yourself through each unavoidable setback in life, get back up, and develop into an even greater person.

The Value of Self-Control

Are you considering the significance of it or the reasons behind it? Imagine that you woke up feeling exhausted and unwilling to move. Simply lying in bed and allowing your thoughts to wander until you lose all control and decide to get out of bed, but you still won't feel good about what you've done. We are all human, after all, and nobody in the world has ever felt horrible when they wake up. While developing self-discipline won't prohibit you from experiencing bad emotions occasionally, it will provide you with a strong advantage to overcome them and find happiness. It is the strength that will allow you to persevere through hardships, withstand temptation, and maintain moral behavior in the face of adversity.

Being disciplined allows you to be free. You might exclaim, "Hey, buddy! Freedom does not equate to denying the desire to consume a cigarette. I can do whatever I want when I'm free. Yes, there are conditions associated with that quotation. Consider this: even though you are attempting to stop smoking, you might find that your need for cigarettes is controlling you and that you are unable to live without them. In this scenario, resisting the need to smoke would not seem like liberation. Now, define freedom for me. To light up?Or to reject it? Self-discipline allows you to freely say no to things that obstruct your path to success and yes to things that facilitate it.

Having self-discipline requires you to manage your judgment of right and wrong rather than your emotions, and You will discover how to develop a super-performer mindset in the upcoming chapters, along with many other life-improving skills.

You will learn important components that are necessary to develop self-discipline while reading this book. Since it is best to understand the material before using it, please read this book cover to cover without making any changes and without skipping any chapters, as it is meant to be read sequentially. You can begin taking action and creating the life of your dreams after you have finished reading the book for the first time.

Chapter 11: Developing Self-Control

Everything is doable with only a little self-control, but without it, even the most ordinary and straightforward objective may appear unachievable.

This usually has to do with something that steers you on a positive path or away from a bad one. It is closely associated with the quality of having willpower or the capacity to postpone satisfaction. This implies that the ability to withstand transient temptations is necessary for achieving long-term objectives. It also means that we ought to have emotional self-control and that, in spite of unpleasant emotions, it is possible to maintain composure under pressure. Consequently, willpower is an intentional self-control that necessitates effort and self-control.

Due to our human nature, we frequently find ourselves deficient in self-control or determination. For instance, you may find yourself watching television far beyond midnight, even if you know you have to get up early for work the next day. Alternatively, you may be so determined to start a fitness program that you can't wait for a cheat day to "have a bite" of something that isn't on your diet. Alternatively, you may be advised by your doctor to quit smoking, but the mere sight or scent of a cigarette compels you to give in and find an excuse, which leads to a relapse into the habit.

There are countless more instances, and we have all undoubtedly experienced them. However, in order to successfully integrate a desired behavior through habit stacking, we require a great deal of self-control and determination. It is what makes a man stand out from the crowd and elevates him above mediocrity. People who possess self-control and perseverance will always succeed in their endeavors, even if others have the skills or means to achieve the same.

Establishing the reason for the change is the first step you must take. It must be sufficiently captivating. Let's imagine you choose to give up smoking in order to prevent further health issues. Alternatively, it could be a deeply held interest, such as a lifelong goal to participate professionally in swimming. Whatever the driving force, it needs to be powerful and convincing enough to maintain momentum.

The next step is to track your actions in relation to that objective. It must be something you desire so much that you will stop at nothing to accomplish it.

Willpower is the final element. It is the one item that will have the biggest impact on your ability to complete tasks and move toward your goal. Your success is already guaranteed if you can set specific goals for yourself and work toward them every day; no other factor comes close to matching your sheer willpower. Much like a sturdy structure, it needs a solid base, and you should begin practicing self-discipline well in advance, even before you decide to focus on your objectives.

If you intend to make significant life changes, be aware that failure is a common companion. Overambition can help you become more aggressive and quick-thinking, but it can also result in false hope syndrome. False hope syndrome is the result of having inflated expectations of who you are and what you can achieve. While optimism is admirable, realism is preferable. For instance, let's say you smoke two packs of cigarettes a day, and you intend to quit completely in a week. Although the intention is commendable, most people don't find it realistic.

False hope syndrome makes it challenging for the person to start a habit-stacking journey to meet objectives within the constraints of his available time or resources. People often have very high expectations for their aspirations. Their goal is to accomplish more significant goals more quickly. Though there's nothing wrong with having a broad perspective, it's important to consider everything. Being unaware of the time and resources required to accomplish a task creates the ideal environment for abrupt burnout.

This will ultimately result in giving up. The result is a vicious cycle in which people keep falling prey to the syndrome of repeatedly trying but failing to change who they are. Rather than going all out, PLAN your success as a process, with a steady stream of small steps that will add up to more substantial outcomes.

Willpower is an energy-intensive process that drains all of your resources, including time, drive, interest, and the desire to keep going forward when you're under stress. You might have noticed that during the most stressful times in your life, you tend to indulge in unhealthy and negative habits – overeating or not eating enough, smoking, drinking, or doing any other satisfies of different kinds to feel good. It can be extremely challenging to regain control over and stop these behaviors.

We get a brief sense of fulfillment from completing these tasks, which diverts our attention from the stressful things in our lives. But your willpower is completely consumed by these stress reactions. Stress impedes an individual's ability to regulate their emotions, which makes it challenging to complete the tasks at hand. Therefore, you must focus on lowering your stress levels in order to practice self-discipline effectively.

Dark Psychology In War

Dark psychology techniques are employed to create fear in the enemy, control them, and make it appear pointless for them to fight. Communication during a war is frequently deceptive. The enemy is portrayed as vicious and brutal.

There is more to a war than just fighting. Propaganda and dark tactics are essential components of a war effort. It is widely acknowledged that the most famous war quote is, "Make your enemy surrender without firing in the air."

For example, Genghis Khan purposefully cultivated a reputation for his ruthless cruelty towards his adversaries (Gale 2019, 2019). He achieved this by coming across a large number of walled cities and castles that welcomed him with open arms. Like in the previous example, winning the game without shooting is possible with superior power and encirclement strategies.

The Stuka Siren: Sound as a Negative Psychological Device

Various war tactics exist. Among these combat strategies is the Nazi SiranStuka. It was a light-bomber aircraft with a siren on board. The Nazis had this siren fastened to the plane. The purpose of this was to terrorize the soldiers.

When the enemy heard the sound of the Stuka, they wanted them to think of death and disaster (Seligman 1972).

Mo' Authority, Mo' Deception

The formidable manipulator!

A wealthy nation can employ dark psychology techniques to manipulate public perception of war. One strategy for a government to prevail in the battle of information is modern colonialism.

For instance, a sizable segment of the West considers Israel to be an intruder. How come? Israel owns a majority of the media companies, which explains why. These media sources present the nation as an invader as opposed to a victim. Something Dark in the Air

In wars and battles, many warriors employ dark psychology to their advantage. Wartime elements come in five different varieties.

portraying your nation or self as "good." showing the opposition as "Bad."

Success ought to be clear-cut and simple.

The true cost of the war is unknown. Keep the psychological toll that battle takes hidden.

Saturday: Embracing Everything, Nothing Less

The statements as mentioned earlier indicate a belief that is indicative of self-destructive behavior. Research on human behavior as a whole demonstrates that life is more complex than just winning and losing. The majority of our lives are spent in the gray area between these two extremes, and if you ignore this, you'll miss out on some incredibly amazing moments.

The prevailing but nonsensical, mindset of "Accepting No Less Than Everything" is connected to everything we have covered so far. It's time to reframe your beliefs if you think that there is no such thing as partial success. The first step in accomplishing your goals is to set milestones. An effective way to conceptualize this is to picture the following situation: As you get closer to finishing the stage in a game, you can save at specific checkpoints. Using milestones will help you avoid the feeling of "sudden death," where failure results in the campaign's termination. As a result, you'll feel more secure and accomplished.

Exercise No. 6: Imagining

One well-known method for practicing self-discipline is visualization, and the best part about it is that you're already doing it. Every time you reflect on the past, consider the present, or dream about the future, you are engaging in it. You are using it more than fifty times a day on purpose.

You have to build vivid, sense-based ideas before you can visualize something in your mind. For instance, you want to wake up two hours earlier than usual so that you can play sports. Start your daily visualizations a week or two prior to the real transformation. Your phone's alarm sounds. Imagine yourself getting out of bed and stretching. As you step into the shower, enjoy the breeze. Finally, picture yourself carrying out the workout.

To help you visualize, focus on the details and visualize the process several times so that it becomes ingrained in your memory. Even a few seconds of visualization can have a significant impact; thirty minutes or more is preferable.

Ways to Avoid Temptation in Your Everyday Lives

Since our decisions determine everything in life, we must maintain our motivation and focus until we succeed. Every day, we are tempted, and this can take us away from our objectives and successes. Overspending, overeating, and overdrinking can cause a number of problems in our lives and keep us occupied with activities that divert our attention from our objectives and cloud our judgment. Therefore, we must learn how to withstand temptation and stick to our life's purpose and goals.

Put Yourself Apart

Temptation can entice us to follow mindlessly into things that seem wonderful, but we need to exercise self-control, divert our attention, and think of something else instead. Many things in life can divert your attention, but if you have self-control and willpower, you can list the many things that are important to you and ensure that you never have to give in to temptation. For example, if your goal is to lose weight, avoid eating at establishments that serve junk food. Even if you do go, be sure to occupy your mind with other pressing matters and come up with something else to think about.

Observe Your Plans

If you have set plans, make sure you follow through on them no matter what. Avoid giving in to temptation and changing your mind. At first, it can be difficult to resist temptations. This is the time when you need to be stronger because if you give in once, you'll always give in. Always create plans that will help you stay motivated to carry out your goals and remain steadfast in your life's ambitions.

Keep Busy

You should keep yourself occupied if you think you succumb to temptation readily. As a result, you never truly have time to sit down and consider what might entice you. Organizing your routine so that you have a few minutes to yourself before calling it a day is a better way to handle things. Even though being overly busy can drain your energy, this will at least help you stay motivated and focused so you can move quickly through your schedule and accomplish your objectives.

Engage in Self-Talk

Nobody else can entice you but yourself. Though there are plenty of temptations and diversions in this world, nobody can force you to become distracted if you so choose. You can always talk yourself out of an attraction if it arises. Usually, when you're tempted, you speak to yourself and convince and justify yourself in doing what you want to do. In a similar vein, you can always talk yourself out of doing it wherever you are. For example, you can always convince yourself that you don't have to smoke because it will negatively affect your life if you decide to stop smoking and you see your friends smoking.

Above all, always remember to have fun. With the limited time we have, discipline is supposed to help us live a happier, more fulfilled life.

How Can Willpower Be Ignited in Chapter 5?

Everybody has something they would like to change, and the drive to advance and better oneself is intrinsic. However, when it comes to making a shift, it can be challenging to figure out how to strengthen your resolve and kick bad habits. Additionally, you are more likely to fail than succeed. Your willpower is insufficient for everything you struggle with. Do we have to follow the same behavioral guidelines from the past? Is it possible to strengthen your resolve, improve your self-control, and make lifelong positive changes? Only if you truly want it is it possible. Willpower can be likened to a muscle that gains strength through regular exercise. It has been discovered that we can change and strengthen our resolve while also breaking free from our habits in the process.

How can one strengthen one's resolve and make a variety of significant life changes? These are some of the actions that, if made into routines, can give you excellent outcomes with regard to willpower.

Providing Brain Food

Remember that missing meals has no positive effects on the brain. If you wish to find out how to strengthen your willpower, things could get even worse. The decision-making muscle is the brain. Whether or not your brain receives enough nourishment affects its capacity for making wise decisions. Consuming wholesome proteins, complex carbohydrates, low-glycemic foods, and vegetables on a daily basis will help you avoid experiencing an abrupt drop in blood sugar levels.

Quit maintaining a constant state of diminished willpower.

Lifting weights is an excellent method of developing muscle. But you would only do weights for an hour straight after having to assist a close buddy with moving furniture. Your muscles will become tired from performing well if you do this. You must give your body and muscles time to heal after lifting weights. The same holds for willpower. While practicing self-control is a terrific method to strengthen your willpower, neglecting to give yourself any respite will quickly sap your resolve. Trainers and coaches distinguish between comfort zones and stretch zones when it comes to sports. You can run a mile in 10 minutes with ease.

You will be in your stretch zone if you pick up the pace to complete a mile in nine minutes. However, it is not a smart idea at all if you continue to stay in the stretch zone. There will be a higher chance of injury for you. The same holds for willpower.

focusing on a single change at a time

Increasing motivation and willpower is simple, but it takes time and requires patience. Every day, every one of us has a limited supply of motivation and willpower. You are never able to change everything at once, and you are also never able to drastically alter your life when things are tough. You have to take one objective at a time and start small if you want to see genuine improvement. People occasionally lose up, not because they lack motivation, but rather because they begin to feel overburdened by the enormous amount of goals they have to accomplish. Dividing the objective into manageable chunks and arranging them in a successful line is a fantastic method to approach this. You will feel immensely satisfied and proud of yourself as you accomplish each sub-goal. It will facilitate you in achieving the following sub-objective.

Keeping Away from Temptation

Those with high levels of self-control won't frequently need to use their willpower. Willpower is, hence, abundant and consistent when required.

By not putting yourself in situations where will is necessary and avoiding the traps where temptation lurks, you can increase your level of willpower. It's a common misconception that those with strong willpower utilize it to avoid getting engaged in crises, while those with weaker will use it to escape them. Thus, avoid all those locations that could challenge your resolve. If you find it difficult to resist temptation, try planning for what you will do instead of giving in to the same.

While you are attempting to strengthen your willpower, it is almost impossible to resist temptations. Making bad decisions can be avoided by having a plan. For example, if you know that your coworker brings doughnuts on Mondays and you are attempting to follow a diet, what type of strategy can you implement to resist the want to indulge in some of it? You must come up with your strategy and create something you are certain would be beneficial.

Forming Robust Yet Compact Habits

Good habits have been shown to benefit you in a number of ways as you develop stronger willpower. Making your bed is a rather basic place to start, but even that small action can have a big impact on your ability to maintain willpower. It occurs as a result of the tiny practices that cultivate self-discipline and self-control. It permeates other facets of your existence.

Being Oneself

It would take a great deal of work on your part to try to repress your typical personality, habits, or preferences. That attempting to do so can weaken willpower is not surprising. It has been observed that those who consistently uphold their aims and ambitions are more resilient to exhaustion than those who tend to exercise such gentle self-control in order to please others. When it comes to willpower, those who constantly strive to win over others may find themselves at a disadvantage compared to those who are confident and at ease with who they are.

Contemplating Something Else

You can block unpleasant thoughts from entering your mind by using your imagination. Every time anything that makes you nervous enters your mind, you will need to teach yourself to think on something else. Let's say you're afraid of the water. Consider traveling by road the next time you are on the water. The idea is to focus on something nice and calming to help you work through any unwelcome thoughts that could otherwise invade your mind. You will benefit if you do not question the effectiveness of this simple method.

Creating an Appropriate To-Do List

Whether it is on paper or not, everyone has a to-do list. Unbeknownst to you, a productivity tool like that makes you more stressed and weakens your resolve. The subconscious will constantly remind you to finish duties because you tend to make endless lists and leave things undone or incomplete. Instead of taking action, you find yourself worrying about it more. You'll start to feel down as you go along. Your emotional condition begins to interfere with your capacity to avoid temptation. Thus, make an effort to keep your to-do list concise and doable. Overcrowding the list will weaken your resolve and is not a long-term solution at all.

Ways To Respond To Failure

Nobody desires failure. Nobody wants to live with the constant fear of not living up to expectations, and failing is the surest path to that point. When you don't succeed, you probably feel bad about yourself, like you're not good enough, or that you've demonstrated something important, like you weren't capable or deserving in the first place.

Unfortunately, one of those things that is unavoidable is failure. When you will ultimately fail at anything, it is more important than if you will fail at all. Since none of us are flawless, everyone makes mistakes from time to time, and that's okay. Self-discipline is neither a means of encouraging perfection nor a means of teaching oneself to be perfect. Failing does not have to make you feel guilty. Move on and proudly display your scars because they are a sign that you fought a battle and refused to let it overcome you, which is a powerful sign in and of itself.

When faced with failure, you may find yourself deeply struggling if you are not careful. You might discover that you are hesitant or unable to act in a way that is advantageous to you if you lack the self-discipline to pull yourself out of the failure hole. Failure need not be a death sentence or a declaration that you are incapable of doing anything well; if you so choose, it need not even be a bad thing.

While it is certainly sad and unpleasant to fail, many beneficial aspects of failure may be recognized. Failure need not define you as a person or determine the type of person you are. By exercising self-control, you can finally overcome the negative emotions that accompany failure and use it as a teaching tool to transform it from an indication that you are incapable of succeeding at anything into something constructive.

www.ingramcontent.com/pod-product-compliance
Lightning Source LLC
Chambersburg PA
CBHW052152110526
44591CB00012B/1950